1976

the tragedy of richard II,

THE
Tragedie of King Richard, the second.

The life and times of
Richard II (1367-1400), King of England (1377-1399)
Compared to those of
Richard of America in His Second Administration

By Robert J. Myers

WASHINGTON, D.C.
Published by Acropolis Books Ltd.
in the Nation's Capital
1 9 7 3

Printed in the United States of America by
COLORTONE PRESS, Creative Graphics Inc.
Washington, D.C. 20009

Type set in Mallard and Times Roman
by Colortone Typographic Division, Inc.

Library of Congress Catalog Number 73-13017
ISBN 87491-371-3 (cloth)
87491-372-1 (paper)

To Sneakers and Rascal,
Two Pussyfooters
and
Betty and Lynn
and Holly and Tim

On the Moral Similarities
Between the Reign of Richard II in England (1377-1399)
And that of Richard II in America (1968--)

It is written that Richard II of England was a character of contradiction. For example, his lofty theory of kingship makes it difficult for the historian to explain his "extravagant bearing in his prosperity." Shakespeare recounted this tale of Richard II and its unexpected and unhappy ending. Noting the similarities of character in the two Richards, the King of England, and the President of the United States, and their handling of power, we have set forth in Shakespeare's style the history of our own times, for your consideration and entertainment.

introduction

Anyone watching on television Richard M. Nixon's performance as President on the night of April 30, 1973 had to be moved in some way by his speech about the political tragedy called Watergate. In my case I was moved to reread Shakespeare's play *Richard II*, which was originally titled *The Tragedy of Richard II*. The lesson of the two reigns is essentially the same, that is, the problems of the retention of power create a crisis for the ruler. In the case of Richard II of England, he held his throne by arranging for the murder of his uncle, while Richard of America has held on to power through an election campaign that was insensitive to the democratic tradition. The Nixon imperial way has led many journalists to comment about the White House as palace and his staff as courtiers. The Watergate revelations have disclosed the trappings of arbitrary power that characterizes imperial rule.

The tragedy is above all political in the broadest sense. While we are involved with the fate of the two Richards, we are even more caught up with concern about the future of the political entities that they govern. In *Richard II* of England, Richard's cousin Henry Bolingbroke will not ignore the murder which secured Richard's throne, and as a consequence, he is exiled. He returns and deposes Richard II, troubled that his usurpation in the end will breed new disasters. In the second administration of Richard of America, the overkill in the electoral process succeeds, but this triumph is tarnished by the Watergate revelations. Those cast in the background are now

11

emerging and gaining strength, as the courtiers fall. Whether there is a Bolingbroke who will put Nixon aside is an open question, but the resolution of that problem is not essential to this story, which is a satire in the style and general plot of the original Shakespeare play, substituting one court for another. The purpose is to demonstrate the parallels of history, the verities of political life, and to display the character of our current set of public political figures. In sum, this satire deals with the ends and means relationship then and now. The plot imperfectly follows that of Shakespeare in this fictionalized account of the times of Richard Nixon. The result, in the words of Victor Gold, Vice-president Agnew's former press secretary, is an "outrageous fabrication," for your entertainment.

R.J.M.

cast of characters

King Richard

Queen Pat

Princess Tricia

Richard's advisors: Lord Haldeman

Lord Ehrlichman

Bishop of Graham

Sir John Dean

Lord Kissinger

Duke Agnew

Agnew's advisors: Sir Victor of Gold

Sir George of Bush

Sir Charles of Percy

Two gardeners

Assorted soldiers

The Clangbird

1. King Richard **2.** Queen Pat **3.** Lord Haldeman **4.** Sir John Dean **5.** Lord Kissinger **6.** Lord Ehrlichman **7.** Bishop of Graham

THE TRAGEDY OF RICHARD II

ABOUT SHAKESPEARE'S RICHARD II

Shakespeare's play of Richard II deals with the last two years of Richard's reign.

Myers' version deals with Richard's second term as the play opens. Shakespeare's Richard II opens with preparations for trial by combat between the Duke of Hereford (Bolingbroke) and the Duke of Norfolk (Mowbray). Richard stops the contest, banishes them both and confiscates the estates to which the Duke of Hereford would have become heir. The Duke of Hereford claims the King's estates in Ireland by force. The King's supporters prove faithless and Richard submits to the Duke of Hereford (Bolingbroke) who arrests him and is killed by his jailers in the Tower of London (Pomfret Castle, in the play) as he tries to escape. The Duke of Hereford succeeds to the throne as Henry IV.

ACT I

SCENE ONE

King Richard in a merry mood in the oval office following his second coronation. The assembled are being instructed on the philosophy and tone of the second administration. Those present: Queen Pat and Princess Tricia; Duke Agnew, apparently the heir apparent; Lord Haldeman and Lord Ehrlichman.

King Richard:

Welcome, my lords and gracious ladies, now's
The hour of cool reflection, parties stilled
And battle-tested legions rest. We hailed
The hordes of our well-wishers, brave
Battalions from the brutal war of fall.   5
I've called you all before our presence
To set the tone for our administration, safe
From blows of our mad adversary, now for all
Intent and purpose, slain, Sir George McGovern,
A pool of curdled milk and rancid honey, not   10
A man of stealth and steel who rules our land
From times historic, but a man of weakness and
Disorder. So spoke our people, and their voice
Is sovereign, be it well remembered, by those
Who dare to challenge the great
And awesome victory of the King.

Lord Haldeman:

Quite so, King Richard, pray enlighten your keen
Supporters, so they in turn can spread the word
To each outpost of this our sacred land.

Duke Agnew:

The reconciliation of the mass of people with   20
Our Gracious style of government, the blending of
The royal and the plain, the kingly style in democratic robes,
Is best of all the forms of government since times
Of Aristotle, nay before, when rude philosophers
Resided on highest mountain peaks, the better to commune
With bulbs of Brightness which thus far have guided
Our mutual destiny.

King Richard:

Philosophy is nigh the root of our broad reign
Throughout this prosperous land.
The droll practitioneers of money grabbing (Rockefeller if
I've leave to speak in confidence fraternal) have
Been banished from the white halls of
Our palace (if I use the proper word)
For as we know, the winnowing of language down
To the last adverb's one of my projects. I take
Some satisfaction that I was the first to call
The War Department by its name:
Defense Department suits our kingly democratic form
No other phrase rings so respected. As for
Your bold description of our reign I welcome, Lord Agnew.
I thank you from the bottom of
The royal heart. Perception is
The characteristic of the right to rule.
Mark well the points of deference, hierarchy too.

KING RICHARD

Those matters are the right of kings, and
Words like 'mutual' are uttered by the Crown
Alone, by our decision, not by yours.

Duke Agnew:

My Lord, t'was not my aim to speak in such
A way so as to wound you. For my speech
Is blunt, not noted for its sensibility.   50
Unclouded visage is my badge of entry to
The halls of this fair palace, and my heart
Is bail for words what may misspeak themselves.
The mutual force of our grand destiny
My Liege, of which I spoke was but the radiance of
Your mind, your reputation for steadfastness in
Adversity, a fierce addiction to
The Truth, that lights my path in just
And holy work.

25

King Richard:

'Tis not, my Lord, my aim to chide you on   60
Your close familiarity. For certain as
The night and day if I fall short in some
Mysterious way, before assassin's arrow or
A bowl of curdled cottage cheese, that you,
Dear Spiro, are my choice and that of all
Our people in quadrennial poll.
Our leadership prevails. Yet though you have
This privileged place it nonetheless is to
The point that royal and democratic rule
Is more complex than our rude father's thought.   70
For where is there the proper place for blood?
Hereditary right has long succored
The lawful government of all our closest friends,
Whose thought, concern about succession is
As great as ours, perhaps, and right and might
Have made it one. I can't ignore the fact
That young Prince David sits at my own table,

Duke Agnew

26

And has in fact a royal line,
Extending through Dwight Eisenhower, a man
Of love, enshrined in temples of the people's mind.   80
So while our destiny is mutual, as
You spoke, 'tis not so closely wound to cut
The law of reason and renown, in case the just
Demands of this our moist and populous land
Take up a chant for one whose claim to royal post
Cannot be fairly set aside. Mutual our roles
On earth, perhaps, but Heaven's judgement must
Provide an alternate in case of doubt.

Duke Agnew:

Our mutual interest goes beyond
A simple setting of the facts,   90
Of who has chosen our noble path amongst
The wreckage of our late and feeble foe.
T'was you and I, my Liege, whose names
Illuminated lights of gold atop the ballot of

The mass, and while I grant with all my heart
Your mark of Richard won the day,
The humble roll I played, for justice, country, and
Fairness helped clear the field
Of Democrats.

King Richard:

A comrade like yourself is rare indeed
And do not take amiss my indication of
Dim plans that may a difference make in terms
Of my succession. First of all, as you well know,
The chances of a stray assault is well
Nigh gone with my attention to the chores
Of life. I venture not from this firm fastness save
With constant faceless guards, and then indeed
Quick to another fort, no less secure than broods
The House of White. I dwell near sea or mountains in
The utmost silence and secretiveness known in the land.
I'm loved by all my people, not from close
Familiarity. 'Tis that which plays my sense of censure
In your use of 'mutual' to mark a time of politics
And not our normal roles in life.

Lord Ehrlichman:

To join my words of lesser plumage to
The soaring phrase of Richard is my aim.
The disassociation from Duke Agnew is
A course I recommend. Affairs domestic are
The role of but one liege, King Richard.
Dancing partners go their separate ways,
However sweet the music. Duke Agnew's use
Of 'mutual' belies the role of King,
The President, as though King Louis' words

Were stale beyond the grave. 'L'etat, c'est moi'
Is now as then the one true word
Of kingly rule, and not to be defiled
By claims, however close, collaboration of
The kind which might incite the mass to think
Two heads share Richard's crown. The crown is cut
To one close-measured size, and he who deigns   130
To share it is unwise.

Queen Pat:

My Liege and lords, it seems to me that on
This sunny post coronation day we all
Are too much caught about in things
That really matter little if at all.
Our eyes must look beyond this glorious day
Towards '76, the bicentennial of
Our nation that provides the inspiration,
If one's required, to soothe our differences within
This holy house so work of government   140
Goes on. The King does as he bids, and we
In turn do as he bids us.

King Richard:

Enough of observation on this scene.
We all are loved and love each other. Yet
I'm loath to say that one word by itself
Would hardly set me thus to mild wrath,
Duke Agnew. Forms of government indeed
Are our fair course of study. Yet in view
Of your demur about details related to
Our recent win has led to some concern   150
Upon my part that form and not the man
Holds your true interest, and that sounds

Of higher moral vein appear in your own scribes'
Releases, are in fact "replayed," to use
The vulgar word, in captive publications, and
Your careful fulminations and dire threats
Conspire to build your image quite as tall
As mine. So heed my word, Duke Agnew, that
More indiscretions on your part will need
Bring forth my closest glance, and if unchecked,   16
Lead to your woe.

Duke Agnew:

I say again, my Liege, to speak with frankness still
Is one of my vain faults, confess to tell.
This doesn't arise from wile or trickery
But rather from a simple rustic way.
It's true, as you imply, that I have wondered in
My mind, occasionally aloud to friends, if we—
I beg the pardon of your Grace—if it
Required the fatal shove of brave but futile George
Into the bowels of boulder canyon at   17
Mount Rushmore. Could we have simply let him lie,
Instead of going to such lengths of daring to
Assure his bald defeat? So what I say amounts
To this: we fight to win, but in so doing, let
All know the blow is judged to light
Quite fairly. Rumors fresh assail me daily, that
Our overwhelming victory may soon be sour,
Afoul with claims to our undoing,
Grave charges from the Watergate.

Lord Haldeman:

Foul, foul, Duke Agnew, to suggest that all   18
Was not as seen in poor McGovern's sad demise.

30

**❝An honest
tale
speeds best
being plainly
told.❞**

**KING RICHARD III
ACT IV
SCENE 4**

The polls were fair, the votes were cast,
And nothing more or less needs saying. Wagging tongues
Like tails of dogs will soon be sliced, no more
To soil affairs of consequence. They're ours
And ours alone. Remember too that those who
Shed our uniform once danger's past
Run further risk of standing naked when
Again the bugle sounds and rough
Opponents take the field.

Queen Pat:

My Lords, excuse me if you will, I fear
My presence compromises tasks of state
That now intrude upon this joyous scene.
Adieu, King Richard, for a while until
The noon repast is nigh. I hasten now
To set the catsup and the cheese
For just the temperature you please.

[exit Queen Pat]

King Richard:

Duke Agnew, let me say again that even in
The inner walls of this wide Open President,
You must take care in talk of politics
To blur the vision of raw power that
My lords all take for granted. Shield the eyes
Of my fair Queen from ugly scenes.
Like other members of our Kingdom she
Cannot with speed sort out the twain of ends
And means, which in our perfect late campaign
Were blended with such flawless skill by nothing less
Than our distinguished Committee to Re-elect the President.
(The acronym of CREEP, however, yet offends the ear.)

32

Duke Agnew:

My Lord's admonishment's well taken if   210
He does indeed mistake my motive. A
Practitioner of arts of office seeking since
My youth I have no second role to play
(save to your Grace) before the holders of
High place in your administration. So
I have the task to say there lurks beneath
The happy acquiescence of the crowd
In dull and idle days of winter, power
To think. As do the people, I reflect
Upon the vastness of our charge,   220
The noble combat we all waged against
The ragged force of crime and passion molded by
Sir George into a fear as black as night,
Of beggars perched upon the chairs in Lincoln's room,
God save our King! Of rule by mobs and worthless votes
In vermin filled and crawly rooms
In chambers of the Capitol Hill.
Great God, even at this time I still at dawn
Wake in a sweat, and pray again for our
Deliverance from fires of Hell, the heat   230
Of which Dante, Himself, could ne'er describe.
Out vile dreams! Yet in those hours when mist
Arises from my native shores, the East
Of Maryland, another mist comes up,
With rancid smell, each day I cross the narrow gap
Twixt House of White and my more modest room—
Without a rug or plated urn for coffee, sans
A carpet, pen and pencil set—foresooth, I lack
The bare essentials of an office for
A civil servant—but enough   240
Of minor inconvenience.

This rancid mist, I say, is what disturbs
Me most as I sit gingerly each day
Upon my worn and squeaky swivel chair.
The smell arises close at hand, my Liege,
And steams above a stale and fetid pool
Of doubt. The mist condenses like the dew
And then come rivulets, like streams
Of apprehension, waters deep behind the gate
Of this grand White House, spreading in the night   25
With force of flood and threatening inundation to this spot
And make us flee like thieves with what we've got.

Lord Haldeman:

Lord Agnew, stay your false and forked tongue.
Your words of treason shall not blot the beauty of
This room, nor anguish now on this glad day
The Prince, our President.

> > > > > > > *[throws down gauntlet]*

Lord Ehrlichman:

Allow me, Lord, to add my voice to Brother Bob's
Impassioned plea. Duke Agnew has the vapors, true,
For what beyond the lack of sense
Would project lies and calumnies?   26
Foul treason then if madness not suffice.
I add my gauntlet to the floor!

> > > > > *[two gauntlets now on floor]*

King Richard:

Desist, my Lords, from this explosive play.
Do not accept these challenges, Duke Agnew, thrown
However justly. I must weigh this matter. I
Cannot allow division foul to rise

Inside our small and perfect democratic plan.
The work of Watergate is all put down
By sure arrests and punished by the Crown.
Duke Agnew's jests are lack of sleep from fears 270
I know not what. To your physician, brave
Agnew, a month of rest or more, I think,
Will swift restore your own good nature, boyish zest
For trampling o'er the foe. Until you're sound
In mind, I'd say, 'tis not in wisdom time
To make conjectures here that you might on
Regret. 'Tis one for all and all for one
For me the Open President, the finest hour
Of this great land. You surely want to stay
At hand, a leading member of this band, 280
And not on outside looking in, a man
Who plays alone, for games without
A team are naught.

Lord Agnew:
[glowering at Haldeman and Ehrlichman]

Be sure, my Liege, God's help will find a way
To do the very things you love in love
Or law, a new and noble age of honor, peace
With honor, war's disgrace. 'Tis true that my
Poor head is reeling with the weight
Of contradictions, which by leave and rest
Will soon, as you have wisely stated, clear   29
And darker fear will disappear.

Lord Haldeman:

I beg you Lord, my Prince, my Sun the King
That my steel gauntlet stay in place, when next
The traitor Agnew comes this way, again
I force the issue of his false campaign. In truth he is
 The enemy within, as warned against
By Marquis John the Hoover, ghost who now
Should intercede—where is his shade?—and cast
The scoundrel Agnew into chains.

King Richard:

Hear, hear, my Lords, l must restrain your ire,   30
Much as it pleases me to see, again, your proud
Determination to assure that nothing harms
My person or my post. The office and the man
Are really one, except when it's
Our noble purpose to appear,
Like Hindu mystic, to be more than one!
I sympathize with your desire to deal
With Agnew root and branch, for just today
He showed before us all a sign
Of mental weakness, no, a flaw of character   31

To fret and trouble me, the King,
With nonsense of the late campaign.
All's fair in love and war, and both
Adventures were combined to save
The Kingdom from the foe and love the votes
Of voters fair. It may be so that labors in
The night leave muddy tracks that day
Time work would tidy up. The boots
That would avoid the puddle by the day
Step in the water by the night. Straight is   320
The gate, my Lords, and you as keepers have
The pledge that loyalty's a two way street,
And prospers in the constant use therein.

        [Haldeman and Ehrlichman bow deeply]

Lord Haldeman:

A two way street, my Lord, but what of those
Who take the alley, rakes that denigrate
Their benefactors?

Duke Agnew:
Enough, foul vermin. Now I say, my Lord,
Grant me the chance to tear them limb from limb, right now!

King Richard:

Again I say, Duke Agnew, but be calm.
I fear your illness passes poor.   330
I cannot nonetheless ignore transgressions towards
My own. For this I must have retribution but
In harmony with your high rank. Instead
Of pressing for your jailing, thrown into
A prison dank, I will insist on exile—
One year away! Now this will give you time

37

To ponder and forget your troubles here.
I think it best if you go yonder, far
Into the Maryland hills, among the high
And cloudy mountains, close beside the raging streams.   34
For those will quickly calm your vapors and
Will hasten your return. Mark well, my Lord,
My speech is measured, yes, but still behind
The velvet gaze lies cold and iron decision, if
By chance you break my bond. One year's exile, then,
Good Ted, and think not poor of me. For if
You hold to allegations that befoul
You with the rest, think then your Lord
Poor Richard, weighted down by cares of state,
Has done the only thing that saves you from   35
A cruel and ugly death. Make haste, before
Our temper changes with the wind, which blows
Now from the south, with gusts of rain and twisting clouds
And dangers sweeping o'er the freshness of the land.

[*Duke Agnew bows to Richard and exits; Haldeman and
Ehrlichman bow and smile at each other. Nixon broods after
Agnew, then addresses himself again to the two remaining
lords.*]

King Richard:

And now my Lords, back to your chores while I
Seek solace by myself to think about
The wily Orientals and the rustic Slav.
Only King Richard has the mind to separate
The wheat from chaff on matters dealing with
The universe. Lord Kissinger points, yea does the star,   360
But I alone can plot the course and win
The race. The common folk do but applaud
So far have I removed the world from their
Concern and contemplation. Let them think
The small, my Lords, while we think great. But not
To lose my humble touch, despite my robes
Of purple and my crown of burnished gold,
I will consult at proper time
My man of old, a champion famed by admiration, not
In matters of state power, but in affairs   370
Close to the soul. Refer I to our friend
The Bishop Bill of Graham, a man
Of lofty purpose and fair wit, who can
At each quadrennial trial, deliver votes
In quantity. The Baptist belt has taken to
Our Realm and turned its back on mules and such
That linked it with a sadder time. I will
Occasion this to be a sign for all
Eternity, that though the rules of law
Are set, the course of state is of itself,   380
And those that think some other way will pose
Those questions to the Bishop, who will handle such
Concerns in the most felicitous way. I may
In fact dispatch the Bishop off to see
Duke Agnew well. If Agnew in his bleak
Exile embraced the cloth, the problem solves itself.

Lord Haldeman:

Your Grace knows best the answer to a test
Of strength and we have no occasion e'er
To doubt the outcome of a battle with
Your foe. But if the power of moral suasion should
In any measure drop, then John and I
Both beg you not to turn from asking us
To do the necessary thing
In matters touching near the King.

King Richard:

I thank you for your loyalty, your zeal!
To ever guard the throne. Besides your strength
I will construct more safeguards for the realm.
Duke Agnew aims his charges straight at me and thee.
The time has come to build a second line.
Our offense stalled, if such the case,
A solid stone defense stand high, a wall
Of China near our throne, the long and thoughtful argument
That's not the current champion's reign at stake.
Say nay. But "Office of the President"
The Holy Grail of our two hundred years.
If there are those who'd mock our royal role,
Is there but one who'd scorn the Holy Office Of
Our race, the throne of Lincoln and the rest?
Relax, my Lords, despite the nervous Agnew's tedious words

QUEEN

Whatever revelation stems
From present feeble probes of judges, priests
And scribes, know you full well
There's further strength to our just cause. The torch
We burn is not just ours, the King's,
But also in this world,
The light of all the universe.

[*King Richard dismisses Haldeman and Ehrlichman and ponders and broods and looks out the window.*]

ACT I
(Continued)

SCENE TWO

Richard lunches with his counselors and seeks advice on affairs of state and what to do with Agnew, who is threatening rebellion.

LUNCHEON SCENE:

Setting:
The meal is through, the four participants are sitting at their coffee: King Richard, the Bishop of Graham, Sir John Dean, counsellor, and Lord Kissinger, privy counsellor on matters foreign.

King Richard:

A bowl of cheese of smooth and tender curd
Is surely life's most glorious treat. The key
To health and happy time is surely this: to seek
The things within your grasp, to earn your cheese
By dint of daily toil, to cultivate
The simple tastes, fear God, up hold the law
And order first and last, as set forth in
The Tablets writ in Stone. Take heed, my Lords,
Of all the High Commandments; and you
Shall stay at peace.   10

Bishop Graham:

Well spoken, Gracious Liege, the ruler of
All natural things. I'm loath to say that for
Your Kingly modesty the realms claimed by
The Lord of Light Himself would face

A worthy challenger, for perfect grace
And judgement seldom have conspired at once
To mold a King of Lofty Grace who consecrates
These halls. The Guard of morals of the world,
A sure hand of our justice, all behold!
If virtue slackens in the teeming mass,   20
One knows the consequence—
A fiery sword shoved up their ass!

[*All applaud; the Bishop beams and bows.*]

Sir John Dean:

The words of Bishop Graham reflect my view,
My Liege, that your attendants of the law
Are lax in apeing such advice
In stopping insults to our law. I mean
The Scribes, if there be doubt, that band of drunks
And thieves that shelter in the basement of
The Royal House, like termites burrowing
To undermine the pinnings of our Reign   30
Of Christian Justice. Malice reigns instead.
They will not rest when Justice's done.
The Cuban band in all its zeal was found,
Bare burglary as their indictments read.
Now justice done, the miscreants inside their cells,
This sniffling band of fool and knaves
Bestir themselves again to cloud the land
With lies and lies, besmirch the name
Of justice in this land. I say enough
Of this false liberty, my Liege. With your   40
Consent I'll rally soon a band of loyal men
And strong who'll set upon the beggars as
They drink and snore inside the bowels of this
Our National Home. To paraphrase the words

Of our illustrious guest, the Bishop of Graham,
If they are here within these walls,
And do us down,
God save their souls, cut off their balls!

King Richard:

Advice you give me, Counsellor Dean, is right
In line with what I see to be the wisest course,   50
Save for some technicalities that yet may bar
A quicker path to peace at home and far.
Sir John's investigation of
The case called Watergate has shown beyond
A doubt that motives small prevailed that night,
A prank of some misguided men who, quite
By chance, were known to some who man this fort
In various tasks. The scribes, the judge in this
Affair all take great pain to move the matter on
Even though their motive's clear: to harm the office of   60
The King, to cast aspersion at
My Kingly name, to sap the vitals of
Our strength and make the task for peace
With honor more a job for Sisyphus
No less, to roll the rock of our great plan
Up to the wall and down again, alas.
Yet progress we do make, Lord Henry, thanks to you.

Lord Kissinger:

Success is not my work alone, My Liege.
It comes from your wise policy, which was,
To my surprise, your own decision to raise   70
Me near your royal presence. I a man
Of humble birth and many masters have
The great good fortune to be here, no less

51

At table rich with Grace and Power,
A table at which I have long sought to sit.
And only through your Royal Mind of keen
Perception, wit and power that I am thus,
Basking beneath the Royal Sun. What place
I have with those your slaves and subjects holding to
Your every word I do not know. I have   80
Foresooth made claim that my role
Doth stem in part from their perception of
My task as cowboy, lone and silent, riding into town.
It's me against the world. This crowd applauds,
But as we know, those here at table, that
Is not the hidden real part. For if
We fill the homely tale with full analogy,
Behind the stump with pistol drawn, hides out the sheriff,
Bold Mel of Laird (now gone) and in the sky
Is Brave Bill's Friend, on guard. While here at home,   90
In fortress firm, is our true ruler, Richard Second, nerves
Rubbed raw by trigger itch, but never once
Rebelling from the task of peace for this
And future times. Great Lords, my role is small.
The power I have derives from here, a mirror
Of light that knowest well the Source.

King Richard:

Well spoke, dear Henry, man of state,
Evoker of the purple phrase.
I must in candor know the cold effects
Of lies, insults and worse arising from   100
The Watergate, as they relate to foreign
Acceptance to our will.

52

66 *I count myself in nothing else so happy as in a soul remembering my good friends.* **99**

KING RICHARD II
ACT II
SCENE 3, LINE 46

Lord Kissinger:

In foreign affairs, my royal liege, the rules
Are firm and never bend, that is to say,
Who has the bucks will nine times out of ten
Bring home the deer. If mixing metaphors
Does not offend the royal ear.
If one assumes that in the end the spreading touch
Of Watergate will reach the outward borders of
The court, as long as it's not squarely put
On me or Thee, the fields abroad will yield
Crops of tranquillity. The heathen monsters that
We face are bound not by rules of law
And grace that have enchanted God-chosen land.
In fact conduct too fair is not admired
By those with hands restrained by neither law nor God.
So stay at rest in that regard, my King.
Fear not what else tomorrow's tidings bring.

Bishop Graham:

In all my years of public life,
Revivals here and foreign lands,   120
Not once have these ears heard so clearly spoke
As why God's grace is shining here
And no where else.
If heathen now were under Richard's sway,
And only then would virtue spread.
Protect us from the infidel both far and near.
Stamp out the scribes, I say, fair King, before
This land is lost like heathen shores, and cheats
And liars form firm in bands to cast the stones
Of doubt towards Host and House. To stay that day   130
We will arrange at once for Sunday prayers
'round ham and eggs, an amulet I learned
In youth, a shining omen for a brighter day.

Sir John Dean:

The Bishop's right, my Lord, we must proceed
To stop the ingrates in their tracks
By corporeal and divine design. My own
Investigation shows they lie,
The lackeys of the Lady Graham, the sneering louts
Who urinize the news, creating fiction as
They piss, without a sense of patriot's heart,   140
A true devotion to the good of land,
To this administration grand,
Or to the person of the King who holds,
By noble right and holy worth,
The fate of this fair kingdom's final place,
The best and last hope of mankind.

King Richard:

Well said, Sir John (and to have thought the boy could lie!)
You must make haste with God's good work,
To shake the sordid scribes, to test
Their pusillanimous wavering will.
White House attack! No less than Ron,
To shout them into full and clumsy flight.
Grand jury here and there impaneled soon.
A sot or two impaled as leaders of the worst
The country has produced.
Route from the barrel all worm-infected apples.
The news is bad enough in fact that if
It needs embroider it should be
In brighter hues.
I'll leave this task to you,
Sir John. Relay my words to Haldeman
And Erhlichman, with proper deference to their high
Position. Harness now the power of my
Administration for this o'erdue task.
I'll make low who oppose me, leave
Them maimed and torn right where they fall.
Our patience is exhausted. Go!

[*All arise*]

Bishop Graham:

Spoken like a Royal Christian, Prince of Peace!

Lord Kissinger:

Your firmness is the strength that guides us all.

King Richard:

Another thing. Do not take flight. I must

A final counsel take before we part.
Bishop, our fine tuned team fills me with pride.
Reports from every side confirm domestic art.
Progress with speed and peace in catholic ways.
What sayest thou, oh Bill of Graham, master
Of sheep in far flung meadows, with ear atuned
From listening to the Lord above the daily din.

Bishop Graham:

Excuse, my Lord, my stumbling fashion once
Unwound's exact translation of the 'catholic' word.
For one brief time my heart knew pause, but
Is now again obedient to law.
The fact you have in truth is right, except
For some small sign of agitation that has risen
Along the shores of Maryland.

Sir John:

The traitor Agnew disobeys the royal word!
I'm not surprised. The kindness of our Lord
Is shown again, but this time sterner action must

Be done, in my poor counsel. Seize his goods
On this fair earth, appropriate it by the CREEP.
Whatever sum is now concealed in its deep vaults
Is not enough for all contingency.
Assure the transfer, Lord, by quick dispatch
Into the jungle Baltimore some bold.
Assassins armed with spears who hit a flank
At thirty yards, and down the traitor like
A suckling pig when he appears on rural stump
To speak his lies of crimes
And treasons, all alleging from the Watergate.

Bishop Graham:

Hold, counsellor, with such advice . . .

King Richard:

Indeed, Sir John, not in the presence of his Grace.

Bishop Graham:

My comment, Sire, was simply this.
An archer on that further shore
Would be a better choice. The distance's more
And chance of fleeing great. A spearman after all
Would give improper version whence he came,
And if the traitor lived so much the shame.
Methinks, my Lords, an archer's best.

King Richard:

The Bishop's right, Sir John, in all things of
The soul. Take heed his words and on your way.
Indulgence of my royal sense
Of fairness comes to mean

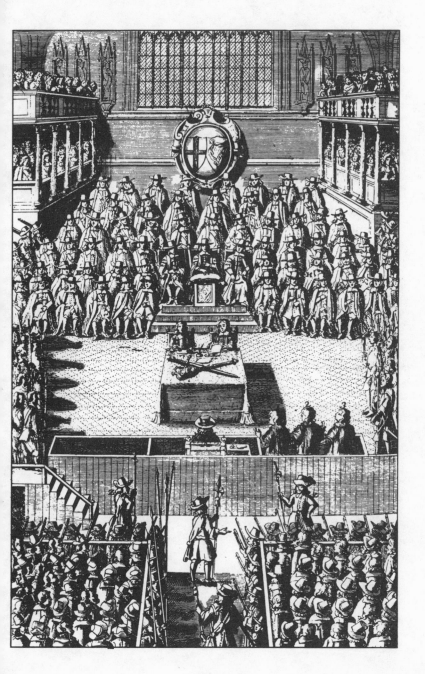

59

Disturbance. Are there other places, Bishop, where
The rebel flag is seen?

Bishop Graham:

My flocks fly far and fast, my Lord, and feed
In every place concerned. The troubles more
In Maryland, but danger lies in this
No less, because that troubled place
Sits near to this your royal capital.
So wing the royal archers well, before
The spore of that infection spreads
To tarnish royal chalice.

Lord Kissinger:

A stitch in time saves nine.

Sir John:

Prevention by the ounce is worth a pound of cure.

King Richard:

Well spoke, my Lords. I'll now retire
To meditate and rest. But lately though
I must confess, my sleep's impaired
By sounds of running water.
The plumbers must make prompt repairs.

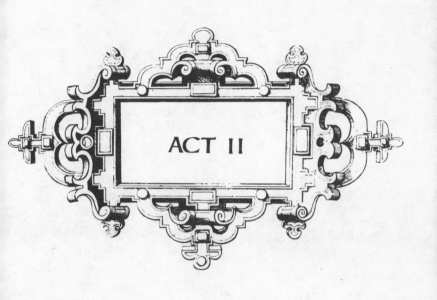

ACT II

SCENE ONE

In Maryland Duke Agnew in exile meets with his advisors.

Duke Agnew:

'Tis two long months of my exile,
So long since I have seen the King,
The soaring monument so near
For me is now so far.
Around his person he is kept
From evil and from good, alas
The one the valet of the other. But
He has no way that he can choose.
The Goths have cut him off as surely as
They walled him in like that poor chap in Poe's   10
Design, the Cask of Amontillado.
(I pride myself on poet's lore
Once having lived in Baltimore,
An easy explanation for Poe's short
And tortured life.) So the King must know
The storms whose noises fill the air
So all who care will see the guilty 'round
The King in this affair of Watergate.
All save the King! All save the King!

Sir Victor:

All save the King? All save the King? My Lord,   20
Your goodness gleams like morning snow,
But common sense confounds your view. I have
Just now sent hungry scribes,
Those overbearing fonts of foolishness,
A letter harsh, exposing Richard's lies.
For not deceived, but a deceiver he,
The fox that joined the hounds.
Beyond that fact the rumors reach my ears
That your estates are seized already.
Assassins prowl throughout this state.   30

A man who scorns a noble Greek
Is not a man for me.

Duke Agnew:

Discretion has not played a role in your
Fast Climb to fame. To criticize
Your tact does not in any mean
Debase your loyalty nor wit.
My fortune seized! My head at stake!
We are in parlous times.
Yet 'til we find our forces great,
We must hold back. For now, just now, it is   40
Our duty sacred, clear to save
The palace from itself, to help King Richard stay
The course, or else be faced with rank
Rebellion, ugly deeds. Refrain I say.
My preference is to aid the King.
If that is not to be I'll think again.
My lands and life are very dear to me.
If mortar hardens on one side,
It hardens on the other.

Sir George of Bush:

It gives me pleasure, noble Duke, to find   50
Safe passage to your fort, however small
And rustic it may be. A base
Is needed if the day be saved from all
Who now surround King Richard, hold him there.
As much a prisoner as if he wore
The novel suit of white and black, a chain
And shackle tied to either foot.
I vouch for Victor's tale of treachery
As it pertains to breath and life.
The time cries out for help.   60

Sir Victor:

We shall expire unless the proper means
Are seized to purify that castle air,
To put the falsifiers hard to rest,
Allow the process self-relief. If he
Who pops the boil's the mob, long years of toil
In Agnew's vines will wither with them, sour grapes,
The bitter fruit of bitter soil.
You must, my Lord, rise quickly now before
The loss is irretrievable, as is
Almost the case, if word of spreading guilt   70
And gross corruption that surround the throne
Are true. Me thinks, my Lord, that still not half
Of it has risen, a body drowned that somehow not
The surface reached. A stubborn maggot-ridden hulk
That stays below the surface but
Will rise in all its rotten stench.
The only chance for justice sits upon your brow.
The Lord protect you from untimely end.
I say we gather all the facts as soon

67

As can be done, assemble them before   80
A band of brave impartial lords, and move
Where justice indicates, with slashing strokes
That leave no head connected to its trunk
Where malice hides and evil thoughts reside.

Sir George of Bush:

The risk of violating Richard's edict's large,
But greater risks incur by lack of charge!
Victor of Gold is right again. His reason's sound
And to the point, where we are bound
To rally those of middle kingdom
Who fear encounter when the lances clash   90
And bucklers bend, and burning oil sprays the head.
Not since the days of ancient kings
Have Lords attacked the moat and turrets of
The Palace. Such an undertaking's fraught
With risk, for he who holds that fort
Has bolts of fire and bags of gold.
Complaint director, tax collector
And other symbols great and small. He waves
And threatens far and near. He's not a man
To cringe from use of instruments of suasion   100
Suitable to each occasion. Wrath
Now turned against Lord Agnew, who knows
What fiends he will unleash for sole control
Of this fair land? The stakes are high.
The King is there. He cowers, hot-eyed and fiery bright.
So if we make our move and lose,
We it is who die.

Duke Agnew:

Let me set forth as best I can

68

The situation now at hand. 'Tis safe
To say the burgeoning claims of venal scribes   110
Hew near the line, despite our claims of bastard lies.
Another way: if one must take
One version or another, Richard's view
Is hardest to believe. We know in truth
From our inquiries that the likes
Of Mitchell, Dean and Hans and Fritz,
Unseasoned men of senseless greed, those fools
Who fail the test of public chore, the quest
For votes, the most demanding task of all—
Those men, we know, conspired to beat by tools   120
Both fair, but mainly foul.
The beggar leper George McGovern,
Who on his own, with none to blame but him,
Would hardly found the votes to call
Attention to his name. And yet
The shame is now corruption. Use
Of funds and felons vile besmirch
The very clouds of heaven, not to say
The party's purse, while passing fat,
Seems destined soon to melt away.   130
My Lords, unless we try, against high odds,
To clear the monsters from the gate, restore
Poor Richard to his wits, or else
No way remains our band to keep our place.
Think too in just three years
Our party runs the race!
The banners fly and chargers neigh.
To win again or so it seems to me,
Dear friends. We now must gird our forces, count
On Richard's clearing mind   140
To simplify our task.

❝*O' call back yesterday bid time return!*❞

**KING RICHARD II
ACT III
SCENE 2**

Sir Victor:

To make my consultation full and fair
I have with difficulty said but half
The things need saying now. Duke Agnew's right
Far as he goes, but I am not so sure
As he that Richard's role in this affair
Runs not deeper than ever seen,
That he will try to keep away
From public view and say he has indeed
Been duped, a premise hard to bear.   150
If history teaches truthfully the shame
Is not the King's, for he foreswearing blame,
Is mightier than the truth.
And yet for Richard, take his early win
O'er Helen of Douglas, tabbed "Pink Lady."
I doubt she knew our Richard's point 'til in
Her back 'twas driven. The Checker's speech
Showed us the guile that all my life I've deigned
To follow, with small rewards. I say
It's Richard spins the web and lays the snare   160
In basement dank, a place so peril-wrought
That none but he goes there.
So to the spider, not the web, I say.

Sir George of Bush:

Bold counsel, Victor Gold. Bold words I do avow.
Your skill and Agnew's right will help us win.
Let that our goal be,
To smash the spider as it spins.
But pluck the web to see what insects lie
Inside. Persuade the spider, if we can,
That miscreants dead are all that's asked for now.   170
A simple speech of unctuous tone,

71

The speciality of Richard's own,
Will pour the oil on tossing sea,
And calm the mobs around the Watergate.
They'll rend us all if nothing's done to rid
The web of those so clearly caught.
'Tis strange indeed that Kings and Lords distain
The view that law is made for even play.
That words to this effect pervade our speech.
Yet it is strange. What King has felt   180
He's not the law unto himself, that rules reach
But the lesser lights than he.
All Kings are captives of their words,
And in our future reign, we must pay heed.
Thus will the blackness of forgetfulness
Embrace us all.

Duke Agnew:

The pink sky to the East reminds me, Lords,
The hour's at hand. Delay is not within
Our power, any more than haste. Deliberations reach
A point, beyond 'tis idle talk. Agree   190
We'll ride together with our friends,
Our banners flying, show of friendly force.
Knowing the secret way, directly to the inner room.
Where we will face King Richard. Send
Flying aides, if that's the only way.
Because this insult's gone on long enough,
And sacrifice of some for all is overdue.
We're off. The red sky may an omen be
Of bloody day or tranquil night.
We'll solve the riddle long before the sky   200
Turns dark. Whether these hours will honored be
Or rest in dust and infamy I cannot see.

But if I fall, my Lords, I pray my bones
Will lie in sunny isles from whence I came,
To fight no more.

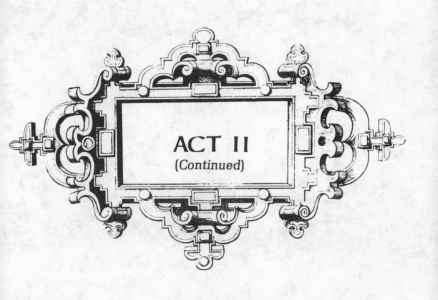

ACT II
(Continued)

Setting:
The Palace. A mob surrounds the moat calling for Richard's abdication, while Agnew leads his trusted men through the secret tunnel.

Lord Haldeman:

Halt varlets, stay! On whose authority
Presume you darkly clothed and hooded band
Of rascals pass my watch into
The Royal Oval room! Desist, I pray, before
I sound the claxon and you reduce to ash
Before the sound has gone. Retreat, I say!
I act to save the King.

Duke Agnew:

Our mission means the King no harm, Lord Haldeman.
Pray treat us not as common thieves.
That we have made our way this far   10
Should convince you of our eminence,
Our right to reach the throne.

> [*Agnew pulls back his mask, as do his two companions,*
> *Sir Victor and Sir George of Bush*].

Lord Haldeman:

'Twould better I should find a pride
Of burglars here than eminence so low and base,
Who somehow wiggled past the guard to reach
This holy place. Stand back, I say, without
Delay. Alarms are ringing on the grounds
And within seconds, succor comes to pin
Your arms and throw your weapons down.

Sir George of Bush:

Your petty threats, dear Haldeman, affect me not.   20
I do not fear your foreign knight.
He fights another battle somewhere else.
Beneath perfumed and silken sheets.

Sir Victor: (drawing his sword)

No harm will come to our King Richard from
This noble band. Our mission is no less
Than rescue from the soiled hands of those
He trusts the most who serve him least. He needs
The best of counsel to undo the harm of yore.
Pray set aside your tinny whistle. Open up the door!

King Richard: (at the open door)

What beast in God's choice Eden makes such sounds   30
Of high alarm? Are guards bereft of reason to
Allow this wretched racket? Here I am
Alone in study, sheltered from all earthly woe.
To ear comes noise and conflict. Must I go
Again to David, camp of peace and quiet
Reflection, just to do God's work?

Lord Haldeman:

A thousand pardons, Lord, but here amongst
Us like the robbers in the night
Stand nobles Gold and Agnew, Bush
The party hack. Ah, now at last arrive 40
The troops in this our inner sanctum. Shoulds't
I have the prisoners beat
With rawhide, shackled by the thumbs and toes?
Or should the soldiers pound them numb
And senseless with a thousand blows?

King Richard:

Had you but acted on your impulse and dealt
With them as you make known, I would not had
To interrupt my work on yellow pad.
Inclined I am to leave them to
The usual fate for those who violate 50
Our rules of confidence. No realm is safe.
Its ruler's life not well secured. Hence all
The locks and doors and traps to hold
The ruler free from harm. It was my fault,
Brave Haldeman, for not changing the plans
Upon Lord Agnew's near exile.
For neither did I think nor fear that the
Foul traitor would come near. But times have changed,
And I will see what at this point he'll offer me.
We are hemmed in, the food is low, and who 60
Knows what we need to stem the mob?
A hank of Victor's curlish hair, forsooth,
Or fatty parts of Bush? Who knows, who knows?
Enter the Oval Office, mark it well.
It should have been the last place you would set
Your evil eyes, in disrespect of royal ban.

How dare you show your face before the Royal gaze!
But out with what you must, Duke Agnew, out
With it I say and do not importune
Me with falsehood. The scurvy scribes have spawned
This mob. I'll not sit still while you
Or others foul the good names of
My closest comrades. Enter Brave Bob
And Jovial John, so that you can yourself
Reject more lies about the rotten Watergate
About which I know nothing. How could
They say that I had knowledge of a sordid plan
To bring an end of factions in this land?
Together yes, rally round the Throne, those are
The words of leaders born to wear
The purple mantle. But my calls
For victory have never meant the cold
Extermination of the other clans.
Opposing factions are the warp and woof
Of our society. The threads that hold
This ancient land compact. My calls
For Sir George's death or worse were just

Hyperbole of war and politics. Pure rhetoric
No more nor less, there is no need for me
To spell in fine detail, Duke Agnew, as   90
You led those bold assaults, just as you now
Provide the charge against the very one
Who gave you birth. Your treachery is hard
To bear, a midwife torn away before
The child has fairly nursed. A double pox
On you, Duke Agnew, for it is your sly
Cohorts who've stoked the fires until
The mob howls for my blood. 'Tis not
Too late in this adventure, substitute
Your blood for mine. The mob cares for the color,   100
Not the source.

Duke Agnew:

Well spoken, Liege, except for one, the mob
That now surrounds the Palace is that flower
I first grew in '68,
And watered by the Watergate. It is
The cultivation of my time. I am its sun.
It will disperse and homeward wend, content again
That this proud house has cleansed itself
Of perfidy. And though your reign is heaven ordained,
The Mandate shakes, as in the East.   110
And if you do not bend your will,
The beast in yonder mob will desecrate these halls.
And neither I nor God nor Bill of Graham
Can save you from most awful fate.

Lord Ehrlichman:

He boasts, my Lord, of power not his own,
Of innuendo of our guilt.
Investigation shows, my King . . .

83

King Richard:

Make haste to strike the royal 'our' from memory.
As who did what to whom those dark
And dreadful days when all my thoughts lay overseas,   12
And I alone fought with the Byzantine,
Until my strength was sapped and I returned
To find support and sustenance in orange
Drenched warmer climes. Speak not of guilt for crimes
Most foul our friends could contemplate,
Not mine. Above all, never implicate
The Royal Crown. The crown of purest gold
Is all in all, the symbol of our perfect peace,
The essence of our kingly way
That's stood well for our land   13
Since Independence Day.

Lord Haldeman:

Without admitting ought, my Lord, it may
Be wise at this conjuncture first to hear
Out Agnew and his men as how they see
This state of peril and what course they might suggest.

                    [*sound of mob getting louder*].

Sir Victor:

Crowned King of fairest land, pray leave
Me set before your noble eyes the fruits
Of my investigation. Here you see
You've been deceived by ones who please to take
Advantage of your fame, who hide behind   14(
The royal robes and slander those who have
One thought, the service to the throne
And country, not for self or hangers-on,
But for the rightful King.

84

Lord Ehrlichman:

That speech, my Lord, 'the nattering nabob of
Negativism,' an embarrassment to the ear
And sense is false. While thick in gross,
That is the paper not the facts, for if
The ink alone were weighed, a feather's worth
Of questioning would overweight the whole.   150

                        [*sound of the mob grows louder*].

King Richard:

Advice like yours, Lord John, is sound enough
In happy times, but from the point of view
Of one whose Crown's at stake, who's fought
Through every odd to earn the name
Of Richard Prudent Pragmatist, this man
Whose every vow is sacrifice to this
Great office, more than vile expediency
Must I consider.
The strength and life of our great constitution, long
Forgot, a matter that has sorely tried   160
My sleep. The constitution and the crown,
My Lords, those who must last whatever else,
And as their guardian I'll give bold Victor voice,
For 'tis my duty, not my choice.

                    [*Richard reads the summary page*].

My Lords, these charges grave and loyally said,
Me thinks, leaves me no doubt, no choice at all.
But now to act without delay to clear
These vapors from the lawns and gardens that
Surround our court, where just beyond the mob's
At bay. I hear the tinkle of the glass.   170
My Lords, think fast!

Lord Ehrlichman:

My King, my life, my very soul, do I
Hear right that with one page of evidence
Untested, unrebuked, you are to throw
Your friends aside, those well known who brought you through
The heavy seas of dangerous waters and set
You safe upon this mighty throne?
Lord Haldeman and Dean, the Bishop Bill,
The rest, should they not be consulted
So this sorry situation, poorly lay,
Will not become calamitous,
A problem worse for all of us?

King Richard:

The easy thing, Lord Ehrlichman, would be
To do just as you say, supported as
I see by Brave Bob's bobbing head. Indeed
The course that you suggest in better times
Would be the one I'd choose. 'Tis but a hundred yards,
You know, from moat to gate and good men run
Almost as fast as sound. But stay, for while
The easy thing is to delay,
To counsel once again the ones who've brought
Me to this fix, honor compels
The hard choice, not the soft. I am dispensed,
Lord Agnew, to proceed directly to
My crowd of loyal subjects, gathered round
Our very house. What should I say, what should I do,
'Ere law and order run askew?

Duke Agnew:

By chance, my Lord, I have a speech
That can be read aloud within the Oval room.

86

**"How long
a time
lies
in one
little
word."**

**KING RICHARD II
ACT I
SCENE 3**

Instruct your men to call the craven scribes to share
This moment and record for history.
Brave Bush of our Grand Party has already placed
The guard, and those foul fellows who've misused
Your confidence bound over to the law.
The way is clear for you to speak.

[*sounds of mob and rocks is louder*].

King Richard:

A speech, my kingdom for a proper speech!

Duke Agnew:

The speech is here, my Lord, in letters large
So that you may without concern pronounce
The words without a lengthy pause, for confidence
To all is high among the virtues you
Possess, to quell the crowd without and hold
The Crown and constitution close within.

[*King Richard sits behind the desk*].

King Richard:

Descendants of this noble land, come round
And listen well while I unfold
A tale of great deception bold,
Of trickery on such a scale, only
A man of total trusting could have had
Such poor assistance, thinking on
Much greater things that those affairs more close
At hand were lost in their design.   220
Most trusted friends, false loyal aides are charged,
You know, with close complicity in Watergate,
A sorry housing project near the walls
Of this our beloved castle. But we know
As truth seeps up, the Watergate became
The symbol of self-serving men,
Integrity, by all commended.
And by clumsy deeds offended.
Now will by all defended.

Last June while scarce at rest from wearying journey from   230
A distant land, then first I heard of deep
Dark business, and to fill my charge, set forth
A full investigation. Now, the CREEPs
Arrested did include but seven of the baser kind,
All friends of John from Mitchell, not to say
That proves his guilt, but just to mind
That nothing more than prankster game was played.
'Till March of this our Lord's best year,
No more did I concern myself with fearful folly.
Then suddenly, like snow in spring,   240
On March 21 new breezes blew, and Hamlet's ghost
Would not lie down again.
I acted quickly, forcefully,

89

To order inquiries properly.
There's some who said I should have known,
But how, I ask you, friends, who's last to know,
If someone's wife is true and where the horns
Are first to sprout?
Despite my haste to run this down,
Precipitous action's not my style.
I want to weigh each tiny word.
Fair justice will be heard. In any case,
That testimony should begin with Dean
And champion Haldeman. I took
The resignation of these men
And cast them on the stake of Justice. If
They're impaled so must it be
And I shall oversee harsh judgement.
I've asked a prosecutor in, to press
The case where it may go. His noble past
Will lead us well, through mysteries that none
Can tell, though none can touch our reign.
And nothing found contemptible remain.

Two questions, friends, we will address to calm
Your fears and superstition. How
Could this have happened, who's to blame?
'Tis true in days far off when I was innocent
In ways of state, then I bestirred
Myself with petty talks from morn to midnight. But
As King I couldn't absorb myself
In menial work, when populations close
And far summoned me to fight
For peace with honor. So as honor beckoned there,
Dishonor beckoned here, but unbeknown.
'Twas just like that, no dark design, yet I
Must bear all burdens, not my own,

And so define responsibility, which rests hard on
Stooped shoulders worn by time, but broad enough,
Mark you all well, to carry still this awful burden.

Enough of this, my loyal friends, much time   280
Is lost in false review of matters now
In willing hands of loyal bands.
Lord Richardson, of high repute, unsheathes his sword
So rest you well. I will again turn full attention to
The dangers elsewhere working round.

My calendar runs down and days flee one by one.
The Lord's work will be done. Of evil I know none.

Duke Agnew:

Spoke like a King, my Lord, let scribes
Write what they will. The curtain's drawn,
The scene must change. Arise, King Richard, meet your fate.   290
The exile you devised for me will fit your case
With certain reservations. Come,
Sir Victor, move him out.

King Richard:

Oh woeful hour that this could come, not
A struggle, not a fight. Lords Haldeman
And Erlichman bound hand and foot.
Learned Henry not at hand to make
Bold rescue of my valiant band.
Duke Connally rides in from the South,
I've heard, in whose command they do not say.   300
Oh shame for this ignominious day!

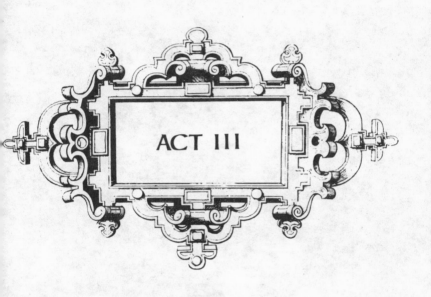

ACT III

Setting:
The Palace garden.
Two gardeners, Queen Pat, and
Princess Tricia.

First Gardener:

The rain last night has soaked the earth and cleared
The air around this place. Or so it seems.
Richard is gone, there's no doubt now. I've peeked
Into his study where a half-filled glass
Of bourbon stands. No pretzels, cheese, or
Cigar. A trace of nothing left.

Second Gardener:

Despite the sun this place makes eerie light.
The mob has gone, thank God, and others clean
The shit and crap from near the site.
But I don't know how this will end. In faith   10
Poor Agnew too is flawed and his
Men butchers like the rest.
Richard was the lawful king, he was.

97

First Gardner:

He was indeed, and that's the rub. For in
His time he so abused the life of law,
Respect for rank, the rest, that his demise
If dead he is, brings low no single flag
Or sounds no muffled drum. 'Tis pity all
Around and who's to pay.

Second Gardener:

The pay goes on and on, you know, through taxes on   20
The poor and winking at the rich.
The system's foul and smells to heaven.
The silence stems, me thinks, from death of hope.
Duke Agnew, well, what's he to care?
King Richard too, in all that's fair, is no
Worse than all other thugs. As to his end,
I'm not so sure. He's held, I'm told, in
His estate, the place in Maryland,
Camp David be his current bed, like floating on
A cloud in outer space.   30

Queen Pat:

So that's the answer to our riddle. Now
We know what we must do. You join your Father quick
As lightning, bind his wounds, he must not be alone.
Determine then what we can do to help restore
Poor Richard to his rightful throne.

Princess Tricia:

Before we flee in our disguises toward
The forests of the West, let's crouch behind
These bushes, thence we learn intelligence

From those rude rustics, better quartered than
Left whole, the kind of spineless cowards that   40
Allowed our Lord to go, protested not.
Oh where resides the pity of the Lord
Who gave them all? Each to his own resources rich.
His wealth his own to wrestle for.
No limits to his aspiration, none
To bar him from this door, save shiftless nature,
Or lack of will or thriftiness. Ingrates of this
Great kingdom well deserve harsh punishment.

First Gardener:

A whisper seems to bow the roses in
This favorite grove of mine. Yet I see naught   50
In deepest shadow, save the conscience on my mind.

Second Gardener:

Your conscience? Fah, I say to you, the whole
Affair makes not a splash. The big concern,
And rightly so, is where the wholesale price
Is at. It goes on up and up like shoots in spring.
So that's the rub and that's the sting.
It nonetheless does trouble me that such a thing
Could happen overnight.
I've long expected such a blow,
But coming from the clowns in brown,   60
The soldiers of the Pentagon.

First Gardener:

Strange as the sky is this affair. Out West
The Duke of Reagan speaks of new elections, new
To Richard or Lord Ted (for that's the name he's now
Affecting, fearful not of some mistake

99

With other more notorious rake).
Duke Wallace in the South begs forth
To parlay with whom ever.
The Lord of Rockefeller pleads for kingdom's unity.
An odd thing that, for e'er has kingdom been   70
So dulled in perfect state of somnolence.

Princess Tricia:

These fools have only blathered bull,
My curses on their sunburned necks.
Mother, let's flee as you suggest to see
What comfort we can give, and what in Hell
There's left to do. Then while you thread
Your way to David, I will call my sister true.
We'll see if Eisenhower, whose name is sacred as
Our own, cannot find soon in some conjunction how
To make a deal with Agnew, and restore   80
The people's faith in Richard's realm.
While no one wants to glory bloodshed in
This tired and reckless race,
In any case we should explore. A war
May be our saving grace.

Queen Pat:

Your Father erred, I fear, sweet Tricia, when
He baited Agnew on blood line
Of royal succession. This, I think,
Moved Agnew's ire, despite the lameness of
The joke, for more than most your poor   90
Dear Father holds the office sacred still,
Annointed by the count of votes (however found,
However dear). Young Eisenhower, I fear's been bought
By Agnew's clever men. They dangle hopes
Of scribbling and if not of poems and essays then
They tease him with a legal course. In truth he'd best
Stay far from devilish complications. Trust
That he lives out his years on his inheritance.
Look not that way for counsel fair and just.
What we can do resides in us, and nowhere else.   100
Remember well my words.

Princess Tricia:

There's nothing left for me but that.

Queen Pat:

Adieu, my love, adieu. See what can raise our fading power,
Through consultation as you say. I make my lonely path
To Richard, 'ere his enemies begin
What evil action not I know, but from
The looks of Agnew and his band, 'twill take
The fire of heaven no less to melt the ice
Around their hearts.

                                        [*Pat and Tricia exit*].

101

Second Gardener:

Look at this rose. The dew falls fresh upon 110
Its face, the same today as yesterday.
I think it matters not to gentle flowers
Who does exert the royal rule.
Yes, wait. Perhaps I see right here a tear
Or two along the leaf. 'Tis well
That something's showing grief. I fear that in
This Eden only serpents show their eyes.
Adam and Eve have flown. Let us manure and lime, then rake.

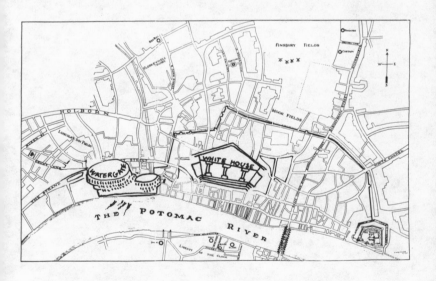

ACT IV

SCENE ONE

The Tower.

King Richard:

Oh torture base and unrelenting, heinous fiends
From cruelist depths, without respect for their
Creator, benefactor, crowned.
How can I bear from day to day
Humiliation so profound?
The weight of robes and scepter press
Me to the ground.

Queen Pat:

Pray Richard, in selfpity set no store.
Your jailors must delight in having more
To add to your discomfort, such as unsigned threats   10
And rumors false that they pass to your ear.
All this is quite unnatural,
And surely 'gainst the rules of war.
They hope to stir up apoplexy. Really, quite a bore.

King Richard:

A bore, dear Pat, a bore, just that, a bore
And nothing more? Our throne's usurped,
The torture's on. The poisonous pen writes bold
And black. The world's asleep. I am not missed.
Dear Pat, my long and lovely Queen,
How has it come to this? We worked, we saved,   20
Collected strings and stamps. Yes, bottle tops.
I wore frayed cuffs and you a good cloth coat.
We've worked hard, Pat, we earned the money, not
For mean or selfish use. Yet they would rob,
Despoil the hive, remove the honey, yet
Have we not made sweet our lives by like industry?

Queen Pat:

Success' measure is its failure. The Watergate,
My Lord, made you o'ershoot the mark.
Your zeal in saving at all cost
The symbol of this royal land,   30
The sacred song, Hail to the Chief,
The panoply of common future, people's grandest dreams,
Went all too well. Whatever name sits on the Throne,
My Lord, becomes the King. Two gardeners inside
Our house revealed to me this simple truth,
Among the flowers placed there by another wife,
Whose industry was great as ours,
Removed before her time by accident.

King Richard:

Your words bore like an awl, dear Pat, the scales
Fall from my eyes. The invocation of   40
Tradition's power seemed but my best defense.
The louts that claimed I launched
A thousand plots from snug inside the Palace
Rooms were hurled back like magic, once
I showed the Crucifix,
The Draculas before me cringed and howled.
I see the flaw, for once the power sets separately,
Who is to say it's not the law that he
Who sits there is the King?

Queen Pat:

Exactly, Lord, except one knows   50
That Watergate and all its findings cast
Aspersion on your Grace. Once legal cards
Are all played out, the mob takes o'er the game.
A subtle transformation, that, complex

For Spiro's brain, yet he now sits
In luxury while we two rest in this damp place.

King Richard:

You're free to go, Pat, free to go. No need
To share this merciless fate. But while I grasp
Your explanation, is it possible that I
Could vanish like the night without   60
A single satrap, beggar, lift a hand
On my behalf? No trace of Lord
Or general saying something kind?
Good God, I handed out the favors fast
As any human can, and yet when things
Are toughest, not a one stands forth in all the land.
Thus, 'All is lost save honor and my life.'

                     [Cell door opens, in steps Sir Charles of Percy]

Sir Charles:

The time has come, King Richard, for an end
To present imprisonment. We'll substitute one prison for
Another. Here to save your head from sharp honed blade   70
Awaits a single Clangbird, up at your command.

King Richard:

A Clangbird here? I thought them long extinct.

Sir Charles:

There is indeed that marvelous bird
Of towering size to fly you off to sunny lands.
Its powerful wings will speed you back and forth
Across the skies, with your full band.
It is the generous deed of Duke Agnew,
The new and future King.

Queen Pat:

There's something I have heard about
The Clangbird's flight that gives me fright.
But to the air, the sun and space
And leave this dreary place.

King Richard:

I find this hard to comprehend,
A speedy transport from this jail?
A jest, proud Percy, that you play
For petty spite?
'Tis true I vowed to block your chance
Of elevation in the court,
But why deceive a helpless King?
You owe me an apology. Why speak of
Clangbirds, gigantic beasts of soaring flight,
Found only in mythology.
Why would you feast on my poor head?

Sir Charles:

Our mission's not for keen revenge,

80

90

112

'Though provocation's surely there.
We'd let your blood if that is needed. For
We too have seen the Word across the sky
Of our great kingdom. 'Office of the King'
Indeed is sacred in our land though not
The holder be. 'Twas your defense   100
In Watergate and much mischief has sprung
From that. No royal bottom on that seat
Can count on personal loyalty. Like whores
In heat, they come and go from that
Once noble throne. Until we change again
The royal rule to rest in one
God-chosen person, one who keeps the state.
We'll deal with most consideration he
Most recent in the place. The head's that next
Would want it so. Compassion modified by fear,   110
The quality of mercy Agnew's reign has brought.

King Richard:

I'm in your power, I'll not protest.
What's there to say? I did my best as God
Told me in language clear, clearer made
By Bishop Graham, a man of God, my closest friend.
Already slain by Agnew's hand, I would portend.

Sir Charles:

The Bishop is a friend of truth,
The foe of all who slight the Royal Office of
The King. He plies again his ancient trade
Of flattering those who need it least.   120
And keeping mindless serfs bemused
By sententious bawling.

King Richard:

Enough, Sir Charles, you must foreswear such blasphemy.
Do what you will. What have you planned?
What is our destiny? Where do we stand?

Sir Victor:

I'm pleased to say Lord Agnew's found a perfect plan,
Sparing your sensibility yet keeping you in hand.
The Clangbird's the carrier of your release.
You and your band will ride on its broad
And roomy back from here to there,
High up from East and West and back. Winter
And summer, your royal court will serve you well.
My Lord will say you've gone abroad. The bulletins
Will issue forth from such and such a clime.
Within a month or so of this, as men forget
And names are blurred, Duke Agnew will assume the throne,
With deep regret.
Our style is bloodless, that's a fact.
Yet we will never take you back.
The endless flying to and fro
Will gently addle morbid mind, and when
The end comes, at last, we'll celebrate the past.

King Richard:

A dirty scheme, foul Victor, but it's what I'd think
You'd do. I'll mount the Clangbird with my group.
Power fancied is the worst of all, a twilight life
I cannot stand. But short of sword to fall on here
I go. The thought of staying near
That rabble, convicts, liars, cheats and crooks
Who let me down—why could they not arrange things more
To near perfection, no loose ends? — offends my sense

114

Of order. Just as beggars are not choosers, nor
Are kings, when all is done. They use the clay
That sticks to them. All in the same thrown pot.
Farewell, then, Percy, Victor too. May you all rot
In hell. Bid Agnew my regards, though dog he is.
The Office of the King alone has life. If no one's there,
Who's to know? Without a herald, who would hear?
I'll muse on that.

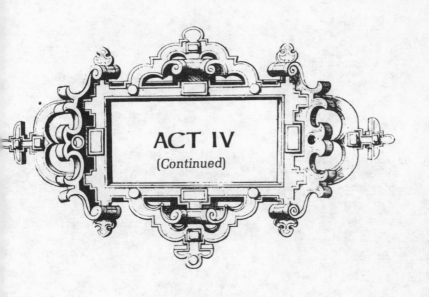

ACT IV

(Continued)

SCENE TWO:

The Palace

Towards evening. The stars are starting to appear, and Sir Charles and Sir Victor are walking towards the Palace to report on the day's doing to Duke Agnew, who is busying himself with plans for his coronation.

Sir Charles:

We've done, I think, exactly what our Liege
Desired. We got them on without a hitch.
The Clangbird's an amazing thing. It flies
An automatic course. It spirals ever higher,
And in tighter rings, until it disappears
Through that wild flight into its ass!
No trace.

Sir Victor:

I well agree the whole affair
Went better than I thought. No tearful scenes,
The whole crew hooked on endless flight.
But one must note, our Lord's instructions were
"To see him off." To certain be that naught
Went wrong, I did conceal a small
Suitcase among the baggage that will surely let
Him off, in case the Clangbird somehow fails.

Sir Charles:

From your bold look, Sir Victor, I know well
You did observe my dallying with
My Lady stewardess, and while she blushed
I too slipped in a powerful pack behind
An empty seat, well calculated to   20
Insure our Guardian's wish.

Sir Victor:

"To see him off" he said indeed, but now
As we approach the lofty halls, perhaps
He meant no more than that, and we
Have witless overstepped his bounds.

121

It may be best if this deed's kept between
Us, Charles, a little secret we can share,
By chance misunderstanding fights with right.
Lord Agnew, hail, we come with firm reports
Of Richard's in the air.

Duke Agnew:

I can then lay aside for now
The dreadful weight of thoughts and work,
Enjoy the moonlight, mark the stars.
For Heaven has laid my course, and done it well.
So here I am today, a simple step
From coronation, legitimizing rule.
Humane exile of Richard and his band
Will grace the spirit of my reign.

Look now upon the coming night. Twin flashes herald
The darkness, omen certain of our right.   40

Sir Charles:

I do foretell the skies will show that your regime
Is heaven blest, the shooting stars pay liege to you.
The moon may lead the rest in awe
To find a heart so true in this
Eternal scheme of things.

Duke Agnew:

Say, look again, the sky seems full
Of falling feathers, seldom seen, falling fast
In endless stream, then out of sight. As well.
There seems to be a vulgar stench.

Sir Victor:

I think the smell is only that   50
Of fetid water. Yonder river's full of slime.
Hold your nose. We should proceed
With all fair haste the day
Of coronation.

Duke Agnew:

And once that's done, I think I shall betake
Myself to native shores, and cleanse my soul
Atop Olympus, mountain of the gods,
A place where I can breathe pure air
And there in cool forgetfulness purge from mind
Anxieties that have plagued me through these days   60
To save the country from itself and Richard.

Sir Charles:

My Liege must keep his talk in democratic phrase,
Lest eager scribes distort your words
And cater to the superstitious mass.

Duke Agnew:

God knows my plan was wrought from motives pure
And well conceived. All have agreed what's done
Is best to save the Office of the King;
No blood was shed and Richard's round the globe.

Sir Victor:

May God his Navigator be!

Duke Agnew:

I am not certain that poor Richard set
Too large a distance from himself, the length
Between the Office of the King
And his own person. Noble office, shrine
Of our religion, Grail of dreams.
Me thinks it's better for the King
To claim the two (the man and institution) one.
This fends off arrows, spears and stones that tough
Contenders sometimes throw. For as it is,
King Richard's gone without lament,
The slightest ripple on the pond of time.
So there's the tale, however sad, but mine.

Sir Victor:

Your explanation fits the facts, but in
This way comes forth the chance of arbitrary rule
Beyond what Richard raised. Forsooth!

Duke Agnew:

Heavy the head that wears the crown. How does
One govern this troubled land? The Curse
Of Power lays o'er the Oval Room.
We go there now to see what lies ahead.

[*sound of fifes and drums playing Yankee Doodle*].

the end

afterword

For those readers whose intellectual appetite has been whetted for more of the original Richard II, we present a series of quotations that may stimulate additional meditation on the politics of modern times.

Look what I speak, my life shall prove it true:
That Mowbray hath received eight thousand nobles
In name of lendings for your Highness' soldiers,
The which he hath detained for lewd employments,
Like a false traitor and injurious villain.

—Henry Bolingbroke (I,i,87-91)

The purest treasure mortal times afford
Is spotless reputation—that away,
Men are but gilded loam, or painted clay.
A jewel in a ten-times-barred-up chest
Is a bold spirit in a loyal breast;
Mine honor is my life, both grow in one;
Take honor from me, and my life is done.

—Thomas Mowbray, Duke of Norfolk (I,i,77-83)

Teach thy necessity to reason thus:
There is no virtue like necessity.
Think not the King did banish thee,
But thou the King. . . .
Go, say I sent thee forth to purchase honor.

—John of Gaunt, Duke of Lancaster (I,iii,276-281)

Ah, Richard! With the eyes of heavy mind
I see thy glory like a shooting star
Fall to the base earth from the firmament;
Thy sun sets weeping in the lowly west,
Witnessing storms to come, woe and unrest;
Thy friends are fled to wait upon thy foes,
And crossly to thy good all fortune goes.

—Earl of Salisbury (II,iv,18-24)

The King is not himself, but basely led
By flatterers; and what they will inform
Merely in hate 'gainst any of us all.

—The Earl of Northumberland (II,i,241-243)

127

The commons hath he pilled with grievous taxes
And quite lost their hearts. The nobles hath he fined
For ancient quarrels and quite lost their hearts.

—Lord Ross (II,i,259-262)

Reproach and dissolution hangeth over him.

—Lord Northumberland (II,i,258)

If I know how or which way to order these affairs,
Thus disorderly thrust into my hands,
Never believe me. Both are my kinsmen.
Th' one is my sovereign, whom both my oath
And duty bids defend; t'other again
Is my kinsman, whom the King hath wronged,
Whom conscience and my kindred bids to right.

—Edmund, Duke of York (II,ii,109-115)

It may be I will go with you, but yet I'll pause,
For I am loath to break our country's laws.

—Edmund, Duke of York (II, iii,167-168)

What must the King do now? Must he submit?
The King shall do it. Must he be deposed?
The King shall be contented. Must he lose
The name of king? a God's name, let it go.

—King Richard the Second (III,iii,142-145)